FAVORITE BRAND NAME

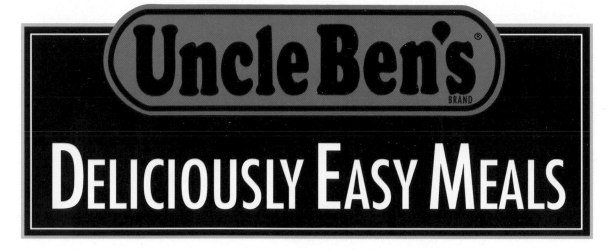

Uncle Ben's®
BRAND

DELICIOUSLY EASY MEALS

PiL

Publications International, Ltd.

Recipe Development: Dari Carré; Mary Holloway; Cheryl Chrysler and Elizabeth Matlin, FoodWorks℠. Recipes approved by the Uncle Ben's, Inc. Recipe Development Center.

Nutritional Analysis: Linda R. Yoakam, M.S., R.D., L.D.

Photography: Peter Walters Photography—Chicago
Photographers: Peter Walters, Kathy Watt
Photographers' Assistant: Jason Imber
Prop Stylist: Sally Grimes
Assistant Prop Stylist: Lisa Wright
Food Stylists: Moisette McNerney, Carol Parik, Mary-Helen Steindler
Assistant Food Stylist: Cindy Melin

Pictured on the front cover: Roasted Turkey Breast with Cherry & Apple Rice Stuffing *(page 46)*.

Pictured on the back cover *(clockwise from top)*: Shrimp and Rice Salad *(page 84)*, Mediterranean Cornish Hen *(page 26)* and Rice and Chicken Wraps *(page 88)*.

ISBN: 0-7853-3351-7

Manufactured in U.S.A.

8 7 6 5 4 3 2 1

Nutritional Analysis: Nutritional information is given for the recipes in this publication. Each analysis is based on the food items in the ingredient list, except ingredients labeled as "optional" or "for garnish." When more than one ingredient choice is listed, the first ingredient is used for analysis. If a range for the amount of an ingredient is given, the nutritional analysis is based on the lowest amount. Foods offered as "serve with" suggestions are not included in the analysis unless otherwise stated.

Microwave Cooking: Microwave ovens vary in wattage. Use the cooking times as guidelines and check for doneness before adding more time.

Uncle Ben's® BRAND

CONTENTS

Introduction   **6**

One-Dish Dinners   **8**

Easy Entertaining   **26**

Kid-Pleasing Meals   **52**

Make It Meatless   **66**

Low-Fat Options   **78**

Index   **92**

Uncle Ben's®
BRAND

INTRODUCTION

With today's busy lifestyle, everyone is looking for quick, easy meal ideas. What's the secret to creating tempting, nutritious meals that your family will love, but take no time to prepare? UNCLE BEN'S® Brand Rice.

Over fifty years ago, Uncle Ben's revolutionized the rice industry with a unique new process that led to the development of UNCLE BEN'S® CONVERTED® Brand Rice. Unlike ordinary rice, Uncle Ben's steams the vitamins and minerals from the outer bran layer into the center of the grain before it is milled. As a result, UNCLE BEN'S® Brand Rice is more naturally nutritious than other brands and cooks up separate, not sticky. **Perfect Every Time**.

All over the world, people are using rice as the main ingredient in entrées, side dishes, appetizers and desserts. It's versatile, naturally fat free and high in energy-boosting complex carbohydrates.

With UNCLE BEN'S® Brand, there's a rice for every meal and occasion. We invite you to try our tantalizing recipes and soon you will discover that great meals can be easy. Just begin with UNCLE BEN'S® Brand Rice. **Perfect Every Time**.

UNCLE BEN'S® CONVERTED® Brand Rice

Our most popular rice and the basis for a wide range of tasty dishes. It's the gold standard of long grain parboiled white rice. Perfect results every time.

UNCLE BEN'S® Brand Instant Rice

No cooking! Add boiling water, set it aside and our instant rice is ready to eat in only 5 minutes. When you have no time to cook, but don't want to sacrifice quality, choose UNCLE BEN'S® Brand Instant Rice.

UNCLE BEN'S® Brand Boil-In-Bag Rice

One-step cooking at its best. Our premium white rice is available in convenient, pre-measured bags. Drop it into boiling water and in 10 minutes you'll have just the right amount of fluffy, perfectly cooked rice.

UNCLE BEN'S® Brand Brown Rice

Made from natural whole grains with a hearty, nutty flavor. Healthy and flavorful UNCLE BEN'S® Brand is the only brown rice that cooks up in 30 minutes—one third faster than other brown rice brands. Also available in instant.

UNCLE BEN'S® Brand Flavored Rice Dishes (formerly Country Inn®)

Choose from an array of easy-to-prepare flavored rice dishes filled with savory spices, vegetables, cheeses and sauces. Each one is ready in just 10 minutes.

UNCLE BEN'S® Brand Long Grain & Wild Rice

A blend of the finest long grain rice and highest quality wild rice with 23 herbs and seasonings. This elegant, flavorful rice makes any meal special.

UNCLE BEN'S® Brand Beans & Rice*

Traditional-tasting beans & rice dishes such as Black Beans & Rice and Red Beans & Rice are just a few of the flavors to choose from. They're completely vegetarian and ready to eat in 10 minutes.

UNCLE BEN'S® Brand Hearty Soups*

You and your family can enjoy the taste of homemade soup without the fuss with UNCLE BEN'S® Brand Hearty Soups. Choose from a variety of popular flavors, such as Broccoli Cheese & Rice and Southwest Vegetable—ready to eat in 10 minutes and low in fat.

UNCLE BEN'S® Brand Specialty Rices*

The perfect choice for the experimental cook. Our selection of 100% natural, exotic rices gives a new twist to your favorite recipes.

*Available in limited distribution

Uncle Ben's®
ONE–DISH DINNERS

WILD RICE MEATBALL PRIMAVERA

1 pound ground turkey
½ cup seasoned bread
  crumbs
1 egg, beaten
2 tablespoons oil
1 can (10¾ ounces)
  condensed cream of
  mushroom soup
2 cups water
1 package (16 ounces)
  frozen broccoli
  medley, thawed
1 box UNCLE BEN'S®
  Brand Long Grain and
  Wild Rice Fast
  Cooking Recipe

1. Combine turkey, bread crumbs and egg; mix well. Shape into 1¼- to 1½-inch meatballs (about 20 to 22 meatballs).

2. Heat oil in large skillet over medium-high heat until hot. Cook meatballs 6 to 7 minutes or until brown on all sides. Drain on paper towels.

3. Combine soup and water in skillet; bring to a boil. Add meatballs, vegetables and contents of seasoning packet, reserving rice. Cover; reduce heat and simmer 5 minutes, stirring occasionally.

4. Add reserved rice to skillet; mix well. Cover; cook 5 minutes more or until hot. Remove from heat; stir well. Cover and let stand 5 minutes before serving.

Makes 6 servings

Nutrition Information Per Serving: Calories: 384, Protein: 22 g, Carbohydrate: 36 g, Fat: 18 g, Cholesterol: 76 mg, Sodium: 1175 mg

Wild Rice Meatball Primavera

CAJUN CHICKEN BAYOU

2 cups water
1 can (10 ounces) diced
    tomatoes and green
    chilies, undrained
1 box UNCLE BEN'S®
    Brand Red Beans &
    Rice
2 boneless, skinless
    chicken breasts
    (about 8 ounces)

1. In large skillet, combine water, tomatoes, beans & rice and contents of seasoning packet; mix well.

2. Add chicken. Bring to a boil. Cover; reduce heat and simmer 20 minutes or until chicken is no longer pink in center.

Makes 2 servings

Nutrition Information Per Serving: Calories: 528, Protein: 39 g, Carbohydrate: 81 g, Fat: 5 g, Cholesterol: 69 mg, Sodium: 1992 mg

COOK'S TIP

If you prefer a spicier dish, add hot pepper sauce just before serving.

HEARTY ONE-POT CHICKEN STEW

12 boneless, skinless
    chicken tenderloins,
    cut into 1-inch pieces
1 box UNCLE BEN'S®
    Brand Red Beans &
    Rice
2¼ cups water
1 can (14½ ounces) diced
    tomatoes, undrained
3 red potatoes, unpeeled,
    cut into 1-inch pieces
2 carrots, sliced ½ inch
    thick
1 onion, cut into 1-inch
    pieces

1. In large saucepan, combine chicken, beans & rice, contents of seasoning packet, water, tomatoes, potatoes, carrots and onion. Bring to a boil. Cover; reduce heat and simmer 20 minutes or until vegetables are tender.

Makes 4 servings

Nutrition Information Per Serving: Calories: 387, Protein: 28 g, Carbohydrate: 65 g, Fat: 2 g, Cholesterol: 41 mg, Sodium: 1069 mg

Cajun Chicken Bayou

BURGUNDY BEEF STEW

¾ **pound beef sirloin steak, cut into 1-inch cubes**

1 **cup diagonally sliced carrots**

1 **teaspoon minced garlic**

¼ **cup Burgundy or other dry red wine**

2⅓ **cups canned beef broth**

1 **can (14½ ounces) diced tomatoes, undrained**

1 **box UNCLE BEN'S® Brand Rice Pilaf Dishes**

1 **jar (15 ounces) whole pearl onions, drained**

1. Generously spray large saucepan or Dutch oven with nonstick cooking spray. Heat over high heat until hot. Add beef; cook 2 to 3 minutes or until no longer pink. Stir in carrots, garlic and wine; cook 2 minutes.

2. Add broth, tomatoes, rice and contents of seasoning packet. Bring to a boil. Cover; reduce heat and simmer 10 minutes, stirring occasionally. Add onions; cook 10 minutes more or until rice is tender. Remove from heat and let stand, covered, 5 minutes.

Makes 4 servings

Nutrition Information Per Serving: Calories: 326, Protein: 25 g, Carbohydrate: 44 g, Fat: 5 g, Cholesterol: 49 mg, Sodium: 568 mg

Variation

One 15-ounce can of drained sweet peas and pearl onions can be substituted for the pearl onions.

CHICKEN WELLINGTON

½ cup water

½ teaspoon chicken bouillon granules

½ cup UNCLE BEN'S® Brand Instant Rice

½ cup chopped fresh spinach

¼ cup finely chopped red bell pepper

4 boneless, skinless chicken breasts (about 1 pound)

1 container (8 ounces) refrigerated crescent rolls

1. Heat oven to 375°F. In medium saucepan, combine water and bouillon granules. Bring to a boil; add rice. Remove from heat; let stand 5 minutes. Stir in spinach and bell pepper.

2. Flatten each chicken breast to about ¼-inch thickness by pounding between two pieces of waxed paper. Season with salt and pepper, if desired. Place ¼ of rice mixture on each chicken breast. Roll up, tucking in edges.

3. Divide crescent roll dough into 4 squares. Press each square to measure 6×6 inches. Place chicken in center of each square. Fold dough to enclose chicken; press edges to seal. Place on greased baking sheet, seam side down.

4. Bake 25 to 30 minutes or until golden brown and chicken is no longer pink in center. *Makes 4 servings*

Nutrition Information Per Serving: Calories: 382, Protein: 30 g, Carbohydrate: 38 g, Fat: 11 g, Cholesterol: 69 mg, Sodium: 862 mg

COOK'S TIP

To flatten chicken breasts, pound them with the flat side of a meat mallet or the edge of a sturdy saucer.

BBQ PORK STIR-FRY

1 (2-cup) bag
   UNCLE BEN'S® Brand
   Boil-in-Bag Rice
1 pound whole pork
   tenderloin
1 tablespoon oil
2 teaspoons minced garlic
2 teaspoons minced fresh
   ginger
1 package (16 ounces)
   frozen stir-fry
   vegetable medley
⅔ cup barbecue sauce
2 tablespoons chopped
   cilantro (optional)

1. Cook rice according to package directions.

2. Trim tenderloin of any fat; cut in half lengthwise, then into ¼-inch slices.

3. Heat oil in large skillet over medium-high heat until hot. Add pork, garlic and ginger; cook about 3 minutes or until pork is no longer pink.

4. Add vegetables and ¼ cup water. Cover; cook 3 minutes, stirring occasionally.

5. Stir in barbecue sauce. Cover; reduce heat and simmer 5 to 7 minutes or just until vegetables are tender and pork is cooked through.

6. Serve pork and vegetables over rice. Garnish with chopped cilantro, if desired.

Makes 4 servings

Nutrition Information Per Serving: Calories: 609, Protein: 31 g, Carbohydrate: 96 g, Fat: 10 g, Cholesterol: 65 mg, Sodium: 688 mg

COOK'S TIP

Choose a stir-fry vegetable medley, such as sugar snap peas, carrots, onions and mushrooms for this recipe.

BBQ Pork Stir-Fry

HEARTY BEEF AND MUSHROOM SOUP

¾ pound sirloin beef
   sandwich steak
3 tablespoons butter or
   margarine, divided
1 small onion, chopped
1 package (6 ounces)
   sliced portobello
   mushrooms, cut into
   1-inch chunks
1 large carrot, sliced
1 box UNCLE BEN'S®
   Brand Brown & Wild
   Rice Mushroom
   Recipe
3 cans (14½ ounces each)
   beef broth
1 tablespoon chopped
   parsley

1. Slice beef into 1-inch wide strips; cut strips into 1-inch pieces.

2. Melt 2 tablespoons butter in large saucepan or Dutch oven over medium-high heat. Add onion and mushrooms; cook 2 minutes. Add remaining 1 tablespoon butter, beef and carrot; cook 2 minutes or until beef is no longer pink.

3. Add rice, contents of seasoning packet and broth. Bring to a boil. Cover; reduce heat and simmer 25 minutes or until rice is tender. Stir in parsley just before serving.

Makes 4 (1½-cup) servings

Nutrition Information Per Serving: Calories: 408, Protein: 28 g, Carbohydrate: 36 g, Fat: 15 g, Cholesterol: 74 mg, Sodium: 1999 mg

COOK'S TIP

If sliced portobello mushrooms are not available, substitute 2 medium portobello mushrooms, cut into chunks. Or, substitute 6 ounces button mushrooms, cut into quarters.

CHICKEN DI NAPOLITANO

1 tablespoon olive oil
2 boneless, skinless
   chicken breasts
   (about 8 ounces)
1 can (14½ ounces) diced
   tomatoes, undrained
1¼ cups water
1 box UNCLE BEN'S®
   Brand Rice Pilaf
   Dishes
¼ cup chopped fresh basil
   or 1½ teaspoons
   dried basil leaves

1. Heat oil in large skillet. Add chicken; cook over medium-high heat 8 to 10 minutes or until lightly browned on both sides.

2. Add tomatoes, water, rice and contents of seasoning packet. Bring to a boil. Cover; reduce heat and simmer 15 to 18 minutes or until chicken is no longer pink in center and liquid is absorbed.

3. Stir in basil. Slice chicken and serve over rice. *Makes 2 servings*

Nutrition Information Per Serving: Calories: 540, Protein: 33 g, Carbohydrate: 76 g, Fat: 11 g, Cholesterol: 69 mg, Sodium: 1427 mg

COOK'S TIP

For more flavor, substitute diced tomatoes with Italian herbs or roasted garlic for diced tomatoes.

WILD RICE SHRIMP PAELLA

1½ cups canned chicken broth

2 tablespoons butter or margarine

1/16 teaspoon saffron *or* 1/8 teaspoon turmeric

2 boxes UNCLE BEN'S® Brand Long Grain & Wild Butter & Herb Rice

1 pound medium shrimp, peeled and deveined

1 can (14½ ounces) diced tomatoes, undrained

1 cup frozen green peas, thawed

2 jars (6 ounces each) marinated artichoke hearts, drained

1. Combine broth, butter, saffron and contents of seasoning packets, reserving rice, in large saucepan. Bring to a boil.

2. Add shrimp; cook over medium-high heat 2 minutes or until shrimp turn pink. Remove shrimp with slotted spoon and set aside.

3. Add tomatoes and reserved rice. Bring to a boil. Cover; reduce heat and simmer 15 minutes.

4. Stir in peas; cover and cook 5 minutes. Add artichoke hearts and shrimp; cover and cook 5 minutes or until hot and rice is tender. Let stand 3 minutes before serving.   *Makes 6 servings*

Nutrition Information Per Serving: Calories: 366, Protein: 21 g, Carbohydrate: 53 g, Fat: 10 g, Cholesterol: 133 mg, Sodium: 1580 mg

Wild Rice Shrimp Paella

ITALIAN SAUSAGE AND RICE FRITTATA

7 large eggs
¾ cup milk
½ teaspoon salt
½ pound mild or hot Italian sausage, casing removed and sausage broken into small pieces
1½ cups UNCLE BEN'S® Brand Instant Brown Rice
1 can (14½ ounces) Italian-style stewed tomatoes
¼ teaspoon Italian herb seasoning
1½ cups (6 ounces) shredded Italian cheese blend, divided

1. Whisk together eggs, milk and salt in medium bowl. Set aside.

2. Preheat oven to 325°F. Cook sausage about 7 minutes in 11-inch ovenproof nonstick skillet over high heat until no longer pink.

3. Reduce heat to medium-low. Stir in rice, stewed tomatoes with their juices, breaking up any large pieces, and Italian seasonings. Sprinkle evenly with 1 cup cheese.

4. Pour egg mixture into skillet; stir gently to distribute egg. Cover and cook 15 minutes or until eggs are just set.

5. Remove from heat. Sprinkle remaining ½ cup cheese over frittata. Bake about 10 minutes or until puffed and cheese is melted.

6. Remove skillet from oven. Cover and let stand 5 minutes. Cut into 6 wedges before serving.   *Makes 6 servings*

Nutrition Information Per Serving: Calories: 407, Protein: 26 g, Carbohydrate: 19 g, Fat: 24 g, Cholesterol: 305 mg, Sodium: 852 mg

COOK'S TIP

Choose a blend of shredded mozzarella and provolone for this frittata, or the blend of your choice.

Italian Sausage and Rice Frittata

CLASSIC CHICKEN BISCUIT PIE

12 boneless, skinless chicken tenderloins, cut into 1-inch pieces

4 cups water

2 boxes UNCLE BEN'S® Brand Chicken Rice Dishes

1 can (10¾ ounces) condensed cream of chicken soup

1 bag (1 pound) frozen peas, potatoes and carrots

1 container (12 ounces) refrigerated buttermilk biscuits

1. Heat oven to 400°F. In large saucepan, combine chicken, water, rice, contents of seasoning packets, soup and vegetable mixture; mix well. Bring to a boil. Cover; reduce heat and simmer 10 minutes.

2. Place in 13×9-inch baking pan; top with biscuits.

3. Bake 10 to 12 minutes or until biscuits are golden brown.

Makes 8 to 10 servings

Nutrition Information Per Serving: Calories: 374, Protein: 18 g, Carbohydrate: 64 g, Fat: 6 g, Cholesterol: 25 mg, Sodium: 1533 mg

COOK'S TIP

For individual pot pies, place rice mixture in small ramekins or casseroles. Proceed with recipe as directed.

NORTHWOODS MUSHROOM SWISS MELTS

4 boneless, skinless
  chicken breasts
  (about 1 pound)
3¾ cups water
2 boxes UNCLE BEN'S®
  Brand Long Grain &
  Wild Rice Original
  Recipe
½ cup chopped green bell
  pepper
½ cup chopped red bell
  pepper
1 cup sliced mushrooms
4 slices (1 ounce each)
  Swiss cheese

1. Spray large skillet with nonstick cooking spray. Add chicken; cook over medium-high heat 5 to 7 minutes or until lightly browned on both sides.

2. Add water, rice and contents of seasoning packets. Bring to a boil. Cover; reduce heat and simmer 20 minutes.

3. Stir in bell peppers; sprinkle mushrooms over chicken. Continue cooking, covered, 5 to 8 minutes or until chicken is no longer pink in center.

4. Place cheese over chicken. Remove from heat; let stand, covered, 5 minutes or until cheese is melted.

Makes 4 servings

Nutrition Information Per Serving: Calories: 551, Protein: 43 g, Carbohydrate: 68 g, Fat: 12 g, Cholesterol: 103 mg, Sodium: 1410 mg

WARM MEDITERRANEAN RICE SALAD

1½ cups uncooked **UNCLE BEN'S® CONVERTED® Brand Rice**

2 teaspoons dried basil

½ cup red wine vinaigrette, divided

1 can (6 ounces) solid white tuna in water, drained and flaked

1 cup chopped green bell pepper

1 cup chopped tomato

½ cup diced red onion

½ cup (about 18 to 20) kalamata or pitted black olives

1. Prepare rice according to package directions. Stir basil and about ⅓ cup of vinaigrette into cooked rice.

2. Meanwhile, combine tuna, bell pepper, tomato and red onion in large salad bowl.

3. Add rice mixture to tuna and vegetables in salad bowl. Stir in remaining vinaigrette and olives.

Makes 6 servings

Nutrition Information Per Serving: Calories: 250, Protein: 13 g, Carbohydrate: 44 g, Fat: 2 g, Cholesterol: 0 mg, Sodium: 402 mg

COOK'S TIP

Kalamata olives are a type of Greek olive that have been marinated in wine vinegar. They have a rich, fruity flavor.

Warm Mediterranean Rice Salad

Uncle Ben's
BRAND

EASY ENTERTAINING

MEDITERRANEAN CORNISH HENS

1 cup UNCLE BEN'S®
  Brand Instant Rice
¾ cup chopped fresh
  spinach
¼ cup chopped sun-dried
  tomatoes in oil,
  drained
2 Cornish hens, thawed
  (about 1 pound each)
1 tablespoon butter or
  margarine, melted
1 clove garlic, minced

1. Heat oven to 425°F. Cook rice according to package directions. Stir in spinach and sun-dried tomatoes; cool.

2. Spoon ½ rice mixture into cavity of each hen. Tie drumsticks together with cotton string. Place hens on rack in roasting pan. Combine butter and garlic; brush each hen with garlic butter.

3. Roast 45 to 50 minutes* or until juices run clear, basting occasionally with drippings.   *Makes 2 servings*

If hens weigh over 18 ounces, roast 60 to 70 minutes.

Nutrition Information Per Serving (without skin):
Calories: 476, Protein: 37 g,
Carbohydrate: 44 g, Fat: 16 g,
Cholesterol: 114 mg, Sodium: 209 mg

COOK'S TIP

Do not store garlic in the refrigerator. Garlic heads will keep up to two months if stored in an open container in a dark, cool place. Unpeeled cloves will keep for up to two weeks.

Mediterranean Cornish Hen

GRILLED FISH, VEGETABLE & RICE PACKETS

1 box UNCLE BEN'S®
  Brand Long Grain &
  Wild Rice Original
  Recipe

4 orange roughy or tilapia
  fish fillets (4 ounces
  each)

3 tablespoons olive oil

3 tablespoons balsamic
  vinegar or fresh
  lemon juice

1 medium red bell pepper,
  cut into thin 2-inch
  strips

1 cup thinly sliced zucchini

½ cup thinly sliced red
  onion

8 button mushrooms,
  quartered

1. Prepare rice according to package directions. Divide cooked rice evenly between four 15×12-inch pieces of heavy-duty foil; spread out rice slightly in center of foil. Place 1 fish fillet over each portion of rice; season fish with salt and pepper, if desired.

2. In medium bowl, gradually whisk oil into vinegar until combined. Add vegetables; toss gently until coated. Divide vegetables evenly over fish and rice; drizzle any remaining oil mixture over fish.

3. Seal foil packets by bringing the two long sides together above food and folding down in several tight folds, then tightly fold in the short ends.

4. Place foil packets, seam side up, on grid over medium coals. Grill, covered, 15 to 20 minutes or until fish flakes easily when tested with fork.

Makes 4 servings

Nutrition Information Per Serving: Calories: 359, Protein: 23 g, Carbohydrate: 42 g, Fat: 12 g, Cholesterol: 26 mg, Sodium: 712 mg

COOK'S TIP

Packets can be placed on a baking sheet and baked in a preheated 400°F oven for 20 to 25 minutes or until the fish flakes easily when tested with a fork.

WILD RICE PESTO TIMBALES

1 medium red bell pepper,
   chopped and divided
1½ cups water
1 box UNCLE BEN'S®
   Brand Brown & Wild
   Rice Mushroom
   Recipe
⅓ cup prepared pesto
   sauce
Fresh basil leaves

1. Reserve ¼ cup bell pepper. In medium saucepan, combine remaining bell pepper, water, rice and contents of seasoning packet. Bring to a boil over high heat. Cover; reduce heat to low and simmer 20 minutes. Remove from heat; let stand, covered, 10 minutes.

2. Stir pesto sauce into rice mixture. Divide reserved ¼ cup bell pepper evenly over bottoms of six 6-ounce custard cups. Evenly divide rice mixture between the cups, gently packing it down. Let stand 3 minutes. Invert each custard cup onto dinner plate, shaking gently to release rice. Garnish each timbale with fresh basil leaves.   *Makes 6 servings*

Nutrition Information Per Serving: Calories:162, Protein: 4 g, Carbohydrate: 21 g, Fat: 7 g, Cholesterol: 4 mg, Sodium: 452 mg

Variation

PESTO WILD RICE: Prepare rice mixture as directed, increasing water to 1¾ cups and adding all of the bell pepper to saucepan. Cook as directed, reducing stand time to 5 minutes. Stir in pesto and serve.

RICE & ARTICHOKE PHYLLO TRIANGLES

1 box UNCLE BEN'S®
  Brand Long Grain &
  Wild Butter & Herb
  Rice
1 jar (6½ ounces)
  marinated quartered
  artichokes, drained
  and finely chopped
2 tablespoons grated
  Parmesan cheese
1 tablespoon minced onion
  or 1 green onion with
  top, finely chopped
⅓ cup plain yogurt or sour
  cream
10 sheets frozen phyllo
  dough, thawed

1. Prepare rice according to package directions. Cool completely.

2. Preheat oven to 375°F. In medium bowl, combine cooked rice, artichokes, Parmesan cheese and onion; mix well. Stir in yogurt until well blended.

3. Place one sheet of phyllo dough on a damp kitchen towel. (Keep remaining dough covered.) Lightly spray dough with nonstick cooking spray. Fold dough in half by bringing short sides of dough together; spray lightly with additional cooking spray.

4. Cut dough into four equal strips, each about 3¼ inches wide. For each appetizer, spoon about 1 tablespoon rice mixture onto dough about 1 inch from end of each strip. Fold one corner over filling to make triangle. Continue folding as you would fold a flag to form a triangle that encloses filling. Repeat with remaining dough and filling.

5. Place triangles on greased baking sheets. Spray triangles with nonstick cooking spray. Bake 12 to 15 minutes or until golden brown.

Makes 40 appetizers

Nutrition Information Per Serving: Calories: 34, Protein: 1 g, Carbohydrate: 5 g, Fat: 1 g, Cholesterol: 1 mg, Sodium: 129 mg

COOK'S TIPS

To simplify preparation, the rice mixture can be prepared a day ahead, covered and refrigerated until ready to use. Use a pizza cutter to cut phyllo dough into strips.

Rice & Artichoke Phyllo Triangles

SOUTHWEST PORK & RICE

1½ teaspoons chili powder, divided

¾ teaspoon ground cumin, divided

¾ teaspoon salt, divided

1½ pounds lean boneless pork, cut into 1-inch pieces

1 tablespoon vegetable oil

1 cup UNCLE BEN'S® CONVERTED® Brand Rice

½ cup chopped onion

1 can (14½ ounces) diced tomatoes, undrained

1. In medium bowl, combine 1 teaspoon chili powder, ½ teaspoon cumin, ¼ teaspoon salt and pepper to taste; add pork and toss to coat.

2. In 12-inch skillet, heat oil over medium-high heat until hot. Add pork; cook, stirring occasionally, until browned, about 3 minutes. Remove pork from skillet; set aside.

3. Add rice and onion to skillet; cook and stir 2 minutes or until rice is opaque and onion is translucent. Stir in 1½ cups water, tomatoes, remaining ½ teaspoon chili powder, ½ teaspoon salt, ¼ teaspoon cumin and pepper to taste. Bring to a boil; stir in pork. Cover; reduce heat to low and simmer 25 to 30 minutes or until rice is tender and most of the liquid is absorbed. *Makes 6 servings*

Nutrition Information Per Serving: Calories: 283, Protein: 20 g, Carbohydrate: 30 g, Fat: 9 g, Cholesterol: 50 mg, Sodium: 419 mg

Serving Suggestions

For added flavor, sprinkle with minced fresh cilantro.

Add 1 cup frozen corn and ½ cup chopped green bell pepper to rice mixture with tomatoes; proceed as directed.

5-MINUTE BEEF & ASPARAGUS STIR-FRY

1 box UNCLE BEN'S®
    Brand Brown & Wild
    Rice Mushroom
    Recipe
¼ pound fresh asparagus,
    cut into 1-inch pieces
1 small onion, cut into
    wedges
1 medium red or yellow
    bell pepper, cut into
    strips
1 medium carrot, peeled
    and cut into thin
    diagonal slices
¼ pound deli roast beef
    sliced ¼ inch thick,
    cut into strips
⅓ cup purchased stir-fry
    sauce

1. Prepare rice according to package directions.

2. During the last 5 minutes of cooking, heat large nonstick skillet or wok over medium-high heat. Add remaining ingredients; simmer, stirring occasionally, until the vegetables are crisp-tender and the mixture is hot. Serve over rice.

Makes 2 servings

Nutrition Information Per Serving: Calories: 485, Protein: 30 g, Carbohydrate: 77 g, Fat: 7 g, Cholesterol: 61 mg, Sodium: 2094 mg

GRILLED CARIBBEAN STEAK WITH TROPICAL RICE

1 (1½-pound) flank steak
¼ cup soy sauce
1¼ cups orange juice, divided
1 teaspoon ground ginger
1 can (8 ounces) pineapple chunks in juice
¼ teaspoon ground allspice
1 cup UNCLE BEN'S® CONVERTED® Brand Rice
1 can (11 ounces) mandarin orange segments, drained

1. Place steak in large resealable plastic food storage bag. In small bowl, combine soy sauce, ¼ cup orange juice and ginger; pour over steak. Seal bag, turning to coat steak with marinade. Refrigerate steak, turning bag occasionally, at least 8 or up to 24 hours.

2. Drain pineapple, reserving juice. Combine remaining 1 cup orange juice and pineapple juice in 1-quart glass measure; add enough water to make 2¼ cups liquid.

3. In medium saucepan, combine juice mixture, allspice and salt to taste. Bring to a boil; stir in rice. Cover; reduce heat to low and simmer 20 minutes. Remove from heat and let stand, covered, 5 minutes.

4. Meanwhile, remove steak from marinade; discard marinade. Grill steak 7 minutes on each side for medium or until desired doneness. Cut steak diagonally across the grain into thin slices.

5. Place rice in serving bowl. Stir in pineapple and oranges. Serve with steak.
Makes 6 servings

Nutrition Information Per Serving: Calories: 381, Protein: 33 g, Carbohydrate: 41 g, Fat: 9 g, Cholesterol: 50 mg, Sodium: 284 mg

Serving Suggestion

For an authentic Caribbean touch, add 1 cup diced peeled mango to rice with pineapple chunks and oranges.

Grilled Caribbean Steak with Tropical Rice

CRANBERRY-GLAZED CORNISH HENS WITH WILD RICE

1 box UNCLE BEN'S®
  Brand Long Grain &
  Wild Rice Fast
  Cooking Recipe
½ cup sliced celery
⅓ cup slivered almonds
  (optional)
1 can (8 ounces) jellied
  cranberry sauce,
  divided
4 Cornish hens, thawed
  (about 1 pound each)
2 tablespoons olive oil,
  divided

1. Heat oven to 425°F. Prepare rice according to package directions. Stir in celery, almonds and ½ of cranberry sauce; cool.

2. Spoon about ¾ cup rice mixture into cavity of each hen. Tie drumsticks together with cotton string. Place hens on rack in roasting pan. Brush each hen with some of the oil. Roast 35 to 45 minutes or until juices run clear, basting occasionally with remaining oil.

3. Meanwhile, in small saucepan, heat remaining cranberry sauce until melted. Remove hens from oven; remove and discard string. Spoon cranberry sauce over hens.   *Makes 4 servings*

Nutrition Information Per Serving (without skin):
Calories: 501, Protein: 37 g,
Carbohydrate: 54 g, Fat: 15 g,
Cholesterol: 98 mg, Sodium: 595 mg

WARM SPINACH AND RICE CHICKEN SALAD

1 box UNCLE BEN'S®
   Brand Chicken Rice
   Dishes
2 boneless, skinless
   chicken breasts
   (about 8 ounces)
⅓ cup reduced-fat Italian
   salad dressing,
   divided
4 cups chopped fresh
   spinach
2 plum tomatoes, chopped
¼ cup pitted ripe olives,
   halved

1. Prepare rice according to package directions.

2. Brush chicken with 2 teaspoons salad dressing. Grill or broil 20 to 25 minutes or until chicken is no longer pink in center and juices run clear, turning once. Slice diagonally.

3. Combine hot cooked rice with remaining salad dressing, spinach, tomatoes and olives; stir until spinach is slightly wilted. Place rice mixture on individual serving plates; top with sliced chicken.   *Makes 2 servings*

Nutrition Information Per Serving: Calories: 587, Protein: 38 g, Carbohydrate: 77 g, Fat: 15 g, Cholesterol: 72 mg, Sodium: 2531 mg

COOK'S TIP

To save preparation time, use packaged spinach that has been washed, dried and torn into bite-size pieces.

MONTEREY CHICKEN AND RICE QUICHE

4 boneless, skinless
    chicken tenderloins,
    cut into 1-inch pieces
1¾ cups water
  1 box UNCLE BEN'S®
    Brand Chicken &
    Broccoli Rice Dishes
  1 cup frozen mixed
    vegetables
  1 (9-inch) deep dish
    ready-to-use frozen
    pie crust
  3 eggs
½ cup milk
½ cup (2 ounces) shredded
    Monterey Jack
    cheese

1. Heat oven to 400°F.

2. In large skillet, combine chicken, water, rice, contents of seasoning packet and frozen vegetables. Bring to a boil. Cover; reduce heat and simmer 10 minutes. Spoon mixture into pie crust.

3. In small bowl, beat eggs and milk. Pour over rice mixture in pie crust; top with cheese. Bake 30 to 35 minutes or until knife inserted in center comes out clean. *Makes 6 servings*

Nutrition Information Per Serving: Calories: 334, Protein: 15 g, Carbohydrate: 37 g, Fat: 14 g, Cholesterol: 126 mg, Sodium: 785 mg

Serving Suggestion

A fresh fruit compote of orange sections and green grapes or blueberries is the perfect accompaniment to this delicious quiche.

Monterey Chicken and Rice Quiche

BEEF TENDERLOINS IN WILD MUSHROOM SAUCE

2 boxes UNCLE BEN'S®
Brand Long Grain &
Wild Butter & Herb
Rice
4 bacon slices, cut into
1-inch pieces
4 beef tenderloin steaks
(4 ounces each) *or* 1
pound beef top sirloin
steak, cut into 4
pieces
1 package (4 ounces)
sliced mixed exotic
mushrooms (crimini,
shiitake and oyster)
or button mushrooms
1 cup chopped onions
⅔ cup half-and-half
2 tablespoons Dijon
mustard
2 tablespoons
Worcestershire sauce

1. Prepare rice according to package directions.

2. Meanwhile, cook bacon over medium-high heat in large skillet until crisp; remove bacon from skillet, reserving 1 tablespoon drippings. Drain bacon on paper towels; set aside.

3. Add steaks to drippings in skillet; cook 2 minutes on each side or until browned. Reduce heat to medium; continue to cook steaks 3 to 4 minutes on each side for medium-rare or to desired doneness. Remove steaks from skillet, reserving drippings in skillet; cover steaks to keep warm.

4. Add mushrooms and onions to drippings in skillet; cook and stir over medium heat until tender, about 5 minutes, stirring occasionally.

5. In small bowl, combine half-and-half, mustard and Worcestershire sauce; mix well. Add to skillet with bacon; cook 3 minutes or until sauce thickens, stirring occasionally.

6. Return steaks to skillet. Continue to cook 3 minutes or until hot, turning steaks over once.

7. Season with salt and pepper to taste, if desired. Transfer steaks to serving plates; top with sauce. Serve with rice.

Makes 4 servings

Nutrition Information Per Serving: Calories: 587, Protein: 39 g, Carbohydrate: 70 g, Fat: 18 g, Cholesterol: 87 mg, Sodium: 1624 mg

INDIAN SUMMER CHICKEN AND RICE SALAD

2 cups water
2 cups UNCLE BEN'S®
Brand Instant Rice
½ cup thinly sliced zucchini
½ cup thinly sliced yellow
summer squash
4 boneless, skinless
chicken breasts
(about 1 pound)
⅔ cup creamy Italian salad
dressing, divided
2 tomatoes, chopped

1. Bring water to a boil; add rice, zucchini and summer squash. Remove from heat and let stand 5 minutes. Cool.

2. Meanwhile, brush chicken with 2 tablespoons salad dressing. Grill or broil 20 to 25 minutes or until chicken is no longer pink in center, turning once. Slice diagonally.

3. Combine rice mixture with remaining salad dressing. Place on serving platter. Surround with tomatoes and top with chicken. *Makes 4 servings*

Nutrition Information Per Serving: Calories: 468, Protein: 30 g, Carbohydrate: 47 g, Fat: 17 g, Cholesterol: 69 mg, Sodium: 389 mg

COOK'S TIP

For a lighter salad with less fat, use reduced-fat salad dressing.

THAI SEAFOOD KABOBS WITH SPICY RICE

1 cups UNCLE BEN'S®
   CONVERTED® Brand
   Rice
1 pound medium raw
   shrimp, peeled and
   deveined, with tails
   intact
½ pound bay scallops
¼ cup soy sauce
2 tablespoons sesame oil
1 large red bell pepper,
   cut into 1-inch
   squares
6 green onions with tops,
   cut into 1-inch pieces
½ cup prepared Thai
   peanut sauce*

*Thai peanut sauce can be found in the Asian section of large supermarkets.

1. Cook rice according to package directions.

2. Meanwhile, place shrimp and scallops in medium bowl. Combine soy sauce and sesame oil; pour half of mixture over shellfish, tossing to coat. Let stand 15 minutes. Reserve remaining soy sauce mixture for basting.

3. Alternately thread shrimp, scallops, bell pepper and green onions onto twelve 12-inch metal skewers. Brush with half the reserved soy sauce mixture. Spoon Thai peanut sauce over each skewer, coating evenly. Grill or broil 8 minutes or until shrimp are pink and scallops are opaque, turning and brushing once with remaining soy sauce mixture and Thai peanut sauce.

4. Serve seafood kabobs with rice. Serve immediately.   *Makes 6 servings*

Nutrition Information Per Serving: Calories: 307, Protein: 26 g, Carbohydrate: 34 g, Fat: 8 g, Cholesterol: 133 mg, Sodium: 1681 mg

Serving Suggestion

Stir ¼ cup chopped peanuts into cooked rice and garnish with minced fresh cilantro, if desired.

Thai Seafood Kabobs with Spicy Rice

ASIAN BEEF WRAPS

1 cup UNCLE BEN'S®
    Brand Instant Rice
8 (6-inch) flour tortillas
2 teaspoons seasoned
    stir-fry oil
½ pound thin boneless
    beef sirloin steak, cut
    into 2-inch strips
½ package (16 ounces)
    frozen stir-fry
    peppers and onions
¼ cup stir-fry sauce
2 tablespoons water
¼ cup thinly sliced green
    onions

1. Cook rice according to package directions; keep warm.

2. Heat tortillas according to package directions; keep warm.

3. Heat oil in large skillet over medium-high heat until hot. Add beef; stir-fry 4 minutes or until no longer pink.

4. Add peppers and onions; stir-fry 1 minute. Stir in stir-fry sauce and water. Reduce heat and simmer gently 6 minutes, stirring frequently. Remove from heat.

5. Place ¼ cup cooked rice in center of each tortilla; top with ¼ cup beef mixture and about 1½ teaspoons green onions. Fold in both sides of tortillas; roll up tightly from bottom, keeping filling firmly packed. Slice each wrap diagonally into pieces. *Makes 4 servings*

Nutrition Information Per Serving: Calories: 423, Protein: 20 g, Carbohydrate: 66 g, Fat: 8 g, Cholesterol: 32 mg, Sodium: 405 mg

Serving Suggestion

Chopped peanuts can be sprinkled over the beef filling with the green onions, if desired.

Asian Beef Wraps

ROASTED TURKEY BREAST WITH CHERRY & APPLE RICE STUFFING

3¾ cups water

3 boxes UNCLE BEN'S® Brand Long Grain & Wild Vegetable & Herb Rice

½ cup butter or margarine, divided

½ cup dried red tart cherries

1 large apple, peeled and chopped (about 1 cup)

½ cup sliced almonds, toasted*

1 bone-in turkey breast (5 to 6 pounds)

*To toast almonds, place them on a baking sheet. Bake 10 to 12 minutes in preheated 325°F oven or until golden brown, stirring occasionally.

1. In large saucepan, combine water, rice, contents of seasoning packets, 3 tablespoons butter and cherries. Bring to a boil. Cover; reduce heat to low and simmer 25 minutes or until all water is absorbed. Stir in apple and almonds; set aside.

2. Preheat oven to 325°F. Place turkey breast, skin side down, on rack in roasting pan. Loosely fill breast cavity with rice stuffing. (Place any remaining stuffing in greased baking dish; cover and refrigerate. Bake alongside turkey for 35 to 40 minutes or until heated through.)

3. Place sheet of heavy-duty foil over stuffing, molding it slightly over sides of turkey. Carefully invert turkey, skin side up, on rack. Melt remaining 5 tablespoons butter; brush some of butter over surface of turkey.

4. Roast turkey, uncovered, 1 hour; baste with melted butter. Continue roasting 1¼ to 1¾ hours, basting occasionally with melted butter, until meat thermometer inserted into center of thickest part of turkey breast, not touching bone, registers 170°F. Let turkey stand, covered, 15 minutes before carving.

Makes 6 to 8 servings

Nutrition Information Per Serving: Calories: 720, Protein: 66 g, Carbohydrate: 57 g, Fat: 25 g, Cholesterol: 144 mg, Sodium: 999 mg

ZESTY ISLAND CHICKEN KABOBS

2 boneless, skinless
    chicken breasts
    (about 8 ounces)
1 small orange, cut into
    wedges
¾ cup fresh or canned
    pineapple chunks
½ red bell pepper, cut into
    1-inch pieces
½ green bell pepper, cut
    into 1-inch pieces
⅓ cup teriyaki sauce,
    divided
1 (2-cup) bag
    UNCLE BEN'S® Brand
    Boil-in-Bag Rice

1. Cut chicken into 1-inch pieces. Thread chicken, orange, pineapple, red bell and green bell peppers alternately onto four 10-inch skewers. Brush some of teriyaki sauce over kabobs. Grill or broil kabobs 10 to 15 minutes or until chicken is no longer pink, turning once and brushing occasionally with remaining teriyaki sauce.

2. Meanwhile, prepare rice according to package directions. Serve kabobs over rice. *Makes 2 servings*

Nutrition Information Per Serving: Calories: 337, Protein: 44 g, Carbohydrate: 186 g, Fat: 5 g, Cholesterol: 17 mg, Sodium: 1909 mg

Serving Suggestion

For a tropical touch, serve rice in a pineapple shell and top with kabobs.

HAM & ASPARAGUS BRUNCH BAKE

2 boxes UNCLE BEN'S®
    Brand Long Grain &
    Wild Rice Original
    Recipe
1 pound asparagus, cut
    into 1-inch pieces
    (about 2½ cups)
2 cups chopped ham
1 cup chopped yellow or
    red bell pepper
¼ cup finely chopped red
    onion
1 cup (4 ounces) shredded
    Swiss cheese

1. In large saucepan, prepare rice mixes according to package directions, adding asparagus during the last 5 minutes of cooking.

2. Meanwhile, preheat oven to 350°F. Grease 11×7½-inch baking dish.

3. Remove rice mixture from heat. Add ham, bell pepper and onion; mix well. Place mixture in prepared baking dish; sprinkle with cheese.

4. Bake 25 to 30 minutes or until mixture is heated through.   *Makes 8 servings*

Nutrition Information Per Serving: Calories: 274, Protein: 19 g, Carbohydrate: 36 g, Fat: 7 g, Cholesterol: 36 mg, Sodium: 1145 mg

Variation

Substitute UNCLE BEN'S® Brand Long Grain & Wild Butter & Herb Rice for the Long Grain & Wild Rice Original Recipe.

COOK'S TIP

This dish can be prepared ahead of time through step 3. Cover with foil and refrigerate several hours or overnight. Bake, covered, in preheated 350°F oven for 15 minutes. Remove foil and continue to bake until heated through, about 15 minutes.

Ham & Asparagus Brunch Bake

GRILLED SWORDFISH STEAKS

1 cup UNCLE BEN'S®
    CONVERTED® Brand
    Rice
4 (1-inch-thick) swordfish
    steaks (about 4
    ounces each)
3 tablespoons Caribbean
    jerk seasoning
1 can (8 ounces) crushed
    pineapple in juices,
    drained
⅓ cup chopped macadamia
    nuts
1 tablespoon honey

1. Cook rice according to package directions.

2. During the last 10 minutes of cooking, coat both sides of swordfish steaks with jerk seasoning. Lightly spray grid of preheated grill with nonstick cooking spray. Grill swordfish over medium coals 10 to 12 minutes or until fish flakes easily when tested with fork, turning after 5 minutes.

3. Stir pineapple, nuts and honey into hot cooked rice; serve with fish.

Makes 4 servings

Nutrition Information Per Serving: Calories: 434, Protein: 27 g, Carbohydrate: 51 g, Fat: 13 g, Cholesterol: 45 mg, Sodium: 1005 mg

COOK'S TIP

For a nuttier flavor, macadamia nuts can be toasted. Place nuts in small nonstick skillet and heat over medium-high heat until lightly browned about 5 minutes, stirring occasionally.

SWEET AND SOUR RICE BOWL

2 tablespoons vegetable oil

12 boneless, skinless chicken tenderloins, cut into 1-inch pieces

1 bag (1 pound) fresh stir-fry vegetables

1 can (8 ounces) pineapple chunks, drained and 2 tablespoons juice reserved

1 cup sweet and sour sauce

2 (2-cup) bags UNCLE BEN'S® Brand Boil-in-Bag Rice

½ cup sliced green onions

1. Heat oil in large skillet or wok. Add chicken; cook over medium-high heat 6 to 8 minutes or until lightly browned on both sides.

2. Add vegetables, pineapple and reserved pineapple juice. Cover and cook 5 to 8 minutes or until chicken is no longer pink and vegetables are crisp-tender. Stir in sweet and sour sauce.

3. Meanwhile, cook rice according to package directions; stir in green onions. Serve chicken mixture over rice.

Makes 4 servings

Nutrition Information Per Serving: Calories: 378, Protein: 34 g, Carbohydrate: 187 g, Fat: 9 g, Cholesterol: 13 mg, Sodium: 436 mg

Uncle Ben's®
BRAND

KID-PLEASING MEALS

STUFFED MEXICAN PIZZA PIE

1 pound ground beef
1 large onion, chopped
1 large green bell pepper,
　chopped
1½ cups UNCLE BEN'S®
　Brand Instant Rice
2 cans (14½ ounces each)
　Mexican-style
　stewed tomatoes,
　undrained
⅔ cup water
2 cups (8 ounces)
　shredded Mexican-
　style seasoned
　Monterey Jack-Colby
　cheese blend, divided
1 container (10 ounces)
　refrigerated pizza
　crust dough

1. Preheat oven to 425°F. Spray 13×9-inch baking pan with cooking spray; set aside.

2. Spray large nonstick skillet with nonstick cooking spray; heat over high heat until hot. Add beef, onion and bell pepper; cook and stir 5 minutes or until meat is no longer pink.

3. Add rice, stewed tomatoes and water. Bring to a boil. Pour beef mixture into prepared baking pan. Sprinkle with 1¼ cups cheese and stir until blended.

4. Unroll pizza crust dough on work surface. Place dough in one even layer over mixture in baking pan. Cut 6 to 8 slits in dough with sharp knife. Bake 10 minutes or until crust is lightly browned. Sprinkle top of crust with remaining ¾ cup cheese; continue baking 4 minutes or until cheese is melted and crust is deep golden brown.

5. Let stand 5 minutes before cutting.
Makes 6 servings

Nutrition Information Per Serving: Calories: 555, Protein: 31 g, Carbohydrate: 55 g, Fat: 23 g, Cholesterol: 87 mg, Sodium: 87 mg

Stuffed Mexican Pizza Pie

CHICKEN CASSEROLE OLÉ

12 boneless, skinless
    chicken tenderloins
2 cups water
1 can (15 ounces) mild
    chili beans, undrained
1 cup salsa
½ cup chopped green bell
    pepper
2 cups UNCLE BEN'S®
    Brand Instant Rice
2 cups (8 ounces)
    shredded Mexican
    cheese blend, divided
2 cups bite-size tortilla
    chips

1. Spray large skillet with nonstick cooking spray. Add chicken; cook over medium-high heat 12 to 15 minutes or until lightly browned on both sides and chicken is no longer pink in center.

2. Add water, beans, salsa and bell pepper. Bring to a boil; add rice and 1 cup cheese. Cover; remove from heat and let stand 5 minutes or until liquid is absorbed. Top with tortilla chips and remaining 1 cup cheese; let stand, covered, 3 to 5 minutes or until cheese is melted.   *Makes 6 servings*

Nutrition Information Per Serving: Calories: 522, Protein: 34 g, Carbohydrate: 60 g, Fat: 17 g, Cholesterol: 64 mg, Sodium: 1110 mg

Chicken Casserole Olé

RICE AND VEGGIE CHEESE MEDLEY

2 tablespoons butter or
    margarine
1 small onion, chopped
¾ teaspoon Italian herb
    seasoning, crushed
1 package (10 ounces)
    frozen mixed
    vegetables
1 box UNCLE BEN'S®
    Brand Cheese Rice
    Dishes
1 cup water
1 cup milk
¾ cup (3 ounces) shredded
    pizza cheese blend

1. Melt butter in large skillet over medium-high heat. Add onion and herb seasoning. Cook 3 minutes or until onion is soft.

2. Add vegetables and rice, reserving seasoning packet; cook 2 minutes. Add water, milk and contents of seasoning packet. Bring to a boil. Cover; reduce heat and simmer 10 minutes, stirring occasionally. Remove from heat.

3. Let stand, covered, 5 minutes. Stir in cheese. _Makes 4 servings_

Nutrition Information Per Serving: Calories: 370, Protein: 14 g, Carbohydrate: 46 g, Fat: 15 g, Cholesterol: 42 mg, Sodium: 422 mg

COOK'S TIP

This meatless dish can be served alone or as an accompaniment to baked or grilled chicken.

CHEESY CHICKEN QUESADILLAS

1¾ cups water
1 box UNCLE BEN'S®
    Brand Chicken Rice
    Dishes
1 cup salsa, divided
6 boneless, skinless
    chicken tenderloins,
    cut into 1-inch pieces
6 (8-inch) flour tortillas
¼ cup sliced ripe olives
1¼ cup (5 ounces) shredded
    Mexican cheese blend
⅓ cup sour cream

1. Heat oven to 450°F.

2. In large skillet, combine water, rice, contents of seasoning packet and ½ cup salsa; add chicken. Bring to a boil. Cover; reduce heat and simmer 10 minutes.

3. Spray both sides of tortillas with nonstick cooking spray. Place 3 tortillas on 15×10×1-inch baking pan. Top each tortilla with ⅓ of cooked rice mixture, olives and ⅓ cup cheese. Top with remaining tortillas; sprinkle with remaining ¼ cup cheese.

4. Bake 5 to 7 minutes or until lightly browned. To serve, cut into wedges. Top with remaining ½ cup salsa and sour cream. *Makes 3 servings*

Nutrition Information Per Serving: Calories: 755, Protein: 37 g, Carbohydrate: 87 g, Fat: 29 g, Cholesterol: 84 mg, Sodium: 2196 mg

COOK'S TIP

Monterey Jack cheese can be substituted for the Mexican cheese blend.

SIMPLE STIR-FRY

1 tablespoon vegetable oil
12 boneless, skinless
    chicken tenderloins,
    cut into 1-inch pieces
1 bag (16 ounces) frozen
    stir-fry vegetable mix
2 tablespoons soy sauce
2 tablespoons honey
2 (2-cup) bags
    UNCLE BEN'S® Brand
    Boil-in-Bag Rice

1. Heat oil in large skillet or wok. Add chicken; cook over medium-high heat 6 to 8 minutes or until lightly browned. Add vegetables, soy sauce and honey. Cover and cook 5 to 8 minutes or until chicken is no longer pink in center and vegetables are crisp-tender.

2. Meanwhile, cook rice according to package directions. Serve stir-fry over rice.   *Makes 4 servings*

Nutrition Information Per Serving: Calories: 865, Protein: 34 g, Carbohydrate: 165 g, Fat: 6 g, Cholesterol: 41 mg, Sodium: 749 mg

Simple Stir-Fry

DRUMSTICK & RICE BAKE

1 tablespoon oil
4 chicken drumsticks
    (about 1 pound)
1 medium onion, chopped
1 medium green bell
    pepper, chopped
¼ teaspoon turmeric
1 box UNCLE BEN'S®
    Brand Homestyle
    Chicken & Vegetables
    Rice Dishes
1 can (14½ ounces) diced
    tomatoes, undrained
1¼ cups canned chicken
    broth

1. Heat oil in medium skillet over high heat until hot. Add chicken; cook 6 minutes or until lightly browned on all sides. Add onion and bell pepper; cook and stir 2 minutes.

2. Stir in turmeric, rice, contents of seasoning packet, tomatoes and broth. Bring to a boil. Cover; reduce heat and simmer 17 minutes.

3. Remove from heat and let stand covered 5 minutes. *Makes 4 servings*

Nutrition Information Per Serving: Calories: 339, Protein: 20 g, Carbohydrate: 41 g, Fat: 11 g, Cholesterol: 94 mg, Sodium: 1295 mg

Serving Suggestion

Sprinkle with chopped parsley, if desired, just before serving.

Drumstick & Rice Bake

MEXICAN LASAGNA

2¼ cups water
1 box UNCLE BEN'S®
    Brand Pinto Beans &
    Rice
8 boneless, skinless
    chicken tenderloins
1 can (10 ounces)
    enchilada sauce
3 (9-inch) flour tortillas
1½ cups (6 ounces)
    shredded Monterey
    Jack-Colby cheese

1. Heat oven to 425°F. In large skillet, combine water, beans & rice and contents of seasoning packet; add chicken. Bring to a boil. Cover; reduce heat and simmer 20 minutes or until chicken is no longer pink in center. Remove chicken; shred chicken using two forks or cut into small pieces.

2. Spread ¼ cup enchilada sauce over bottom of 9-inch pie plate. Place 1 tortilla over enchilada sauce. Top with ⅓ each of remaining enchilada sauce, beans & rice, chicken and cheese. Repeat layers twice.

3. Bake 5 to 10 minutes or until hot and bubbly; cut into wedges.

Makes 6 servings

Nutrition Information Per Serving: Calories: 329; Protein: 21 g; Carbohydrate: 38 g; Fat: 10 g; Cholesterol: 43 mg; Sodium: 937 mg

COOK'S TIP

Top with sliced avocado, chopped tomatoes, chopped fresh cilantro or sour cream.

SOUTHERN BBQ CHICKEN AND RICE

1½ cups water
1 cup UNCLE BEN'S® CONVERTED® Brand Rice
1 cup barbecue sauce, divided
4 skinless bone-in chicken breasts
1 package (6 half ears) frozen corn-on-the-cob

1. In large skillet, combine water, rice, ¾ cup barbecue sauce and chicken. Bring to a boil. Cover; reduce heat and simmer 25 minutes. Add corn and continue cooking 15 to 20 minutes or until chicken is no longer pink in center.

2. Spoon remaining ¼ cup barbecue sauce over chicken. Remove from heat; let stand 5 minutes or until liquid is absorbed. *Makes 4 servings*

Nutrition Information Per Serving: Calories: 441, Protein: 23 g, Carbohydrate: 78 g, Fat: 5 g, Cholesterol: 46 mg, Sodium: 969 mg

POCKET MEALS ON THE RUN

8 boneless, skinless chicken tenderloins, cut into 1-inch pieces
1 cup UNCLE BEN'S® Brand Instant Rice
½ cup crumbled feta cheese
⅓ cup oil and vinegar or Italian salad dressing
4 pita breads, halved
1 cup shredded lettuce
2 plum tomatoes, chopped
¼ cup sliced ripe olives

1. Spray large skillet with nonstick cooking spray. Add chicken, cook over medium-high heat 6 to 8 minutes or until lightly browned and no longer pink. Add 1 cup water. Bring to a boil; add rice. Cover; remove from heat and let stand 5 minutes or until liquid is absorbed. Stir in cheese and salad dressing.

2. Fill pita bread halves with lettuce and chicken rice mixture. Top with tomatoes and olives. *Makes 4 servings*

Nutrition Information Per Serving: Calories: 489, Protein: 23 g, Carbohydrate: 60 g, Fat: 19 g, Cholesterol: 40 mg, Sodium: 918 mg

FRIED RICE CAKES

1 package (6 ounces) UNCLE BEN'S® Brand Homestyle Chicken & Vegetables Rice Dishes
⅓ cup thinly sliced green onions, including tops
2 eggs, beaten
2 tablespoons minced fresh cilantro
2 tablespoons soy sauce
1 teaspoon minced fresh ginger
2 to 3 tablespoons vegetable oil, divided

1. Prepare rice according to package directions, omitting butter. Cover; refrigerate until completely chilled. Stir remaining ingredients, except oil, into cold rice.

2. In 12-inch skillet, heat 1 tablespoon oil over medium heat until hot. For each rice cake, place ⅓ cup rice mixture into skillet; flatten slightly to 3-inch diameter. Cook 4 cakes at a time 3 to 4 minutes on each side or until golden brown. Add more oil to skillet as needed.

Makes 4 to 6 servings
(10 to 11 rice cakes)

Nutrition Information Per Serving: Calories: 257, Protein: 8 g, Carbohydrate: 33 g, Fat: 10 g, Cholesterol: 74 mg, Sodium: 651 mg

COOK'S TIP

Rice cakes may be cooked in advance, covered and refrigerated. When ready to serve, place in single layer on baking sheet. Bake, uncovered, in preheated 350°F oven for 10 to 15 minutes or until heated through.

Fried Rice Cakes

Uncle Ben's®
BRAND

MAKE IT MEATLESS

RICE AND CHICK-PEA CHILI

⅔ cup **UNCLE BEN'S®
CONVERTED® Brand
Rice**
1 can (15 ounces) chick-
  peas, undrained
1 can (15 ounces) diced
  tomatoes, undrained
1 can (8 ounces) diced
  green chilies
1 cup frozen corn
¼ cup chopped fresh
  cilantro
1 tablespoon taco
  seasoning
½ cup (2 ounces) shredded
  reduced-fat Cheddar
  cheese

1. In medium saucepan, bring 1¾ cups water and rice to a boil. Cover, reduce heat and simmer 15 minutes.

2. Add remaining ingredients except cheese. Cook over low heat 10 minutes. Serve in bowls sprinkled with cheese.
Makes 4 servings

Nutrition Information Per Serving: Calories: 324, Protein: 13 g, Carbohydrate: 59 g, Fat: 4 g, Cholesterol: 8 mg, Sodium: 1108 mg

Serving Suggestion

To round out the meal, serve this hearty chili with corn bread and fresh fruit.

Rice and Chick-Pea Chili

RICE & VEGETABLE SALAD

1¾ cups water

⅔ cup UNCLE BEN'S® CONVERTED® Brand Rice

1¼ cups sugar snap peas or snow peas

1¼ cups sliced mushrooms

1 cup halved cherry tomatoes

⅓ cup reduced-fat Caesar salad dressing

¼ cup grated Parmesan cheese

1. In medium saucepan, bring water and rice to a boil. Cover; reduce heat and simmer 20 minutes or just until tender.

2. Meanwhile, stem peas and cut in ½-inch lengths. Combine peas and remaining ingredients in large bowl.

3. Rinse cooked rice under cold running water to cool; drain well. Add to vegetable mixture; toss to coat rice with dressing. Serve immediately or chill until ready to serve. *Makes 4 servings*

Nutrition Information Per Serving: Calories: 206, Protein: 8 g, Carbohydrate: 36 g, Fat: 4 g, Cholesterol: 12 mg, Sodium: 252 mg

VEGETARIAN RICE & BLACK BEAN CHILI

2½ cups water

2 cups UNCLE BEN'S® Brand Black Beans & Rice

½ cup thinly sliced carrot

1 small zucchini, quartered lengthwise and sliced

⅓ cup diced red bell pepper

1 can (8 ounces) tomato sauce

½ cup (2 ounces) Cheddar cheese

1. Place water in medium saucepan. Stir in beans & rice and contents of seasoning packet. Bring to a boil. Add carrot. Cover; reduce heat and simmer 10 minutes.

2. Add zucchini and bell pepper. Cover; reduce heat and simmer 5 minutes. Stir in tomato sauce. Cover and simmer 8 to 10 minutes or until rice is tender. Top with cheese. *Makes 4 servings*

Nutrition Information Per Serving: Calories: 409, Protein: 14 g, Carbohydrate: 77 g, Fat: 6 g, Cholesterol: 15 mg, Sodium: 1723 mg

Rice & Vegetable Salad

RICE, CHEESE & BEAN ENCHILADAS

1 (2-cup) bag
    UNCLE BEN'S® Brand
    Boil-in-Bag Rice
4 cups shredded zucchini,
    drained (2 medium)
1 tablespoon reduced-
    sodium taco sauce
    mix
1 can (15 ounces) pinto
    beans, rinsed and
    drained
1 can (10 ounces)
    reduced-fat, reduced-
    sodium cream of
    mushroom soup
1 can (8 ounces) diced
    green chilies
12 (8-inch) flour tortillas
2 cups (8 ounces)
    reduced-fat Mexican
    cheese blend, divided

1. Prepare rice according to package directions.

2. Combine zucchini and taco sauce mix in large nonstick skillet. Cook and stir zucchini 5 minutes. Add beans, soup, chilies and cooked rice. Bring to a boil.

3. Spray 13×9-inch or 12×8-inch microwavable baking dish with nonstick cooking spray. Spoon about ½ cup of rice mixture onto center of each tortilla. Top with 2 tablespoons cheese. Roll up to enclose filling; place in baking dish. Sprinkle remaining cheese over enchiladas. Microwave 4 minutes or until cheese is melted. *Makes 6 servings*

Nutrition Information Per Serving: Calories: 568, Protein: 26 g, Carbohydrate: 87 g, Fat: 12 g, Cholesterol: 21 mg, Sodium: 1552 mg

Serving Suggestion

Serve with sliced mango or orange sections.

Rice, Cheese & Bean Enchilada

QUICK SKILLET QUICHE

4 eggs

⅓ cup 1% milk

2 teaspoons Cajun
    seasoning

1 cup reduced-fat Cheddar
    cheese, divided

1 cup UNCLE BEN'S®
    Brand Instant Rice

1 cup chopped fresh
    asparagus

¾ cup chopped green
    onions

½ cup chopped red bell
    pepper

1. Preheat oven to 350°F. In medium bowl, whisk eggs, milk, Cajun seasoning and ½ cup cheese. Set aside.

2. Cook rice according to package directions.

3. Meanwhile, spray ovenproof medium skillet with nonstick cooking spray. Heat over medium heat until hot. Add asparagus, green onions and bell pepper. Cook and stir 5 minutes. Add cooked rice and mix well.

4. Shape rice mixture to form crust on bottom and halfway up side of skillet. Pour egg mixture over crust. Sprinkle with remaining ½ cup cheese. Cover; cook over medium-low heat 10 minutes or until eggs are nearly set. Transfer skillet to oven and bake 5 minutes or until eggs are completely set.   *Makes 6 servings*

Nutrition Information Per Serving: Calories: 177, Protein: 11 g, Carbohydrate: 19 g, Fat: 6 g, Cholesterol: 153 mg, Sodium: 369 mg

TEX-MEX RICE SALAD

2 cups water
2 cups UNCLE BEN'S®
   Brand Instant Rice
1½ cups chunky-style salsa
1½ cups (6 ounces) reduced-
   fat Mexican cheese
   blend
1 can (15 ounces) red
   beans, rinsed and
   drained
¾ cup chopped fresh
   cilantro

1. Bring water to a boil in medium saucepan. Add rice; cover and remove from heat. Let stand 5 minutes. Rinse cooked rice under cold running water to cool; drain.

2. Combine rice and remaining ingredients until well blended.

Makes 6 servings

Nutrition Information Per Serving: Calories: 306, Protein: 18 g, Carbohydrate: 46 g, Fat: 5 g, Cholesterol: 6 mg, Sodium: 599 mg

Variation

For spicier salad, use medium or hot salsa or add chopped jalapeño pepper.

QUICK FRIED RICE

1 cup UNCLE BEN'S®
   Brand Instant Brown
   Rice
1 tablespoon margarine
½ cup sliced yellow
   summer squash
½ cup diced red bell pepper
½ cup chopped green
   onions with tops
2 eggs, lightly beaten
2 teaspoons soy sauce

1. Cook rice according to package directions.

2. Melt margarine in medium nonstick skillet. Add squash, bell pepper and green onions; cook and stir over medium-low heat 5 minutes. Add eggs; cook and stir 2 minutes just until eggs are cooked.

3. Add cooked rice to vegetable mixture; sprinkle with soy sauce. Cover skillet and cook over low heat 5 minutes or until rice is hot.

Makes 4 servings

Nutrition Information Per Serving: Calories: 253, Protein: 8 g, Carbohydrate: 40 g, Fat: 7 g, Cholesterol: 107 mg, Sodium: 240 mg

GRILLED VEGETABLES & BROWN RICE

1 medium zucchini
1 medium red or yellow pepper, quartered lengthwise
1 small onion, cut crosswise into 1-inch-thick slices
¾ cup Italian dressing
4 cups hot cooked UNCLE BEN'S® Brand Brown Rice

1. Cut zucchini lengthwise into thirds. Place all vegetables in large resealable plastic food storage bag; add dressing. Seal bag; refrigerate several hours or overnight.

2. Remove vegetables from marinade, reserving marinade. Place bell peppers and onions on grill over medium coals; brush with marinade. Grill 5 minutes. Turn vegetables over; add zucchini. Brush with remaining marinade. Continue grilling until vegetables are crisp-tender, about 5 minutes, turning zucchini over after 3 minutes.

3. Remove vegetables from grill; coarsely chop. Add to hot rice; mix lightly. Season with salt and black pepper, if desired.

Makes 6 to 8 servings

Nutrition Information Per Serving: Calories: 302, Protein: 4 g, Carbohydrate: 38 g, Fat: 16 g, Cholesterol: 0 mg, Sodium: 239 mg

COOK'S TIP

Grilling adds a unique smoky flavor to vegetables and brings out their natural sweetness. The easiest way to grill vegetables is to cut them into large pieces and toss them in salad dressing or seasoned oil before grilling. Seasoned raw vegetables may also be wrapped tightly in foil packets and grilled until tender.

Grilled Vegetables & Brown Rice

COOL-AS-A-CUCUMBER SALAD

4 cups cooked
     UNCLE BEN'S®
     CONVERTED® Brand
     Rice
1 cup finely chopped
     seeded cucumber
¾ cup plain yogurt or sour
     cream
2 tablespoons finely
     chopped onion
1 tablespoon balsamic
     vinegar
2 teaspoons dried dill
     weed
1 teaspoon salt
¼ teaspoon black pepper

1. Rinse hot cooked rice under cold running water to cool; drain.

2. In large bowl, combine cooked rice with remaining ingredients; mix well. Cover and refrigerate until well chilled to allow flavors to blend, about 4 hours.

Makes 6 servings

Nutrition Information Per Serving: Calories: 163, Protein: 4 g, Carbohydrate: 33 g, Fat: 1 g, Cholesterol: 3 mg, Sodium: 380 mg

COOK'S TIP

Removing the seeds from a cucumber is easy. Cut it in half lengthwise and scoop out the seeds with a small spoon.

Cool-as-a-Cucumber Salad

Uncle Ben's® BRAND

LOW–FAT OPTIONS

CARIBBEAN PORK KABOBS AND RICE

1 cup UNCLE BEN'S®
  CONVERTED® Brand
  Rice
1½ cups peeled, diced sweet
  potato
2 tablespoons plus 2
  teaspoons Caribbean
  seasoning, divided
1 can (8 ounces) pineapple
  chunks in pineapple
  juice
1 (12-ounce) pork
  tenderloin, cut into
  1½-inch cubes
1 red bell pepper, cut into
  1-inch squares
1 green bell pepper, cut
  into 1-inch squares
¼ cup dry-roasted peanuts

1. In medium pan, heat 2 cups water to a boil. Add rice, sweet potato and 2 teaspoons Caribbean seasoning. Cover, reduce heat and simmer 10 minutes or until rice and sweet potato are tender.

2. Drain pineapple chunks, reserving juice. Add pineapple chunks to rice mixture.

3. Preheat broiler. Place remaining 2 tablespoons Caribbean seasoning into large resealable plastic food storage bag. Add pork; seal bag and turn to coat pork with seasoning. Thread pork and bell peppers onto skewers.

4. Broil kabobs 4 minutes on each side. Turn and brush with reserved pineapple juice. Continue cooking 2 minutes on each side until pork is no longer pink.

5. Top rice with peanuts and serve with kabobs. *Makes 4 servings*

Nutrition Information Per Serving: Calories: 463, Protein: 26 g, Carbohydrate: 72 g, Fat: 8 g, Cholesterol: 49 mg, Sodium: 918 mg

Caribbean Pork Kabobs and Rice

RICE AND TURKEY SKILLET CURRY

2 cups water

1 cup UNCLE BEN'S® CONVERTED® Brand Rice

¾ cup (6 ounces) pineapple juice

⅓ cup diced dried apricots

¼ cup dried cranberries

1 teaspoon curry powder

1½ cups (8 ounces) cooked turkey

1. In large skillet, bring water, rice, pineapple juice, apricots, cranberries and curry powder to a boil. Cover; reduce heat and simmer 15 minutes or until rice is tender and liquid is absorbed.

2. Add turkey to rice. Cover and cook over low heat 5 minutes or until turkey is hot.   *Makes 4 servings*

Nutrition Information Per Serving: Calories: 326, Protein: 21 g, Carbohydrate: 57 g, Fat: 1 g, Cholesterol: 47 mg, Sodium: 34 mg

RICE PILAF WITH FISH FILLETS

1 cup UNCLE BEN'S® CONVERTED® Brand Rice

1 can (14½ ounces) fat-free reduced-sodium chicken broth

1 cup sliced green onions

2 cups sugar snap peas or snow peas

12 ounces Dover sole fillets

¼ cup reduced-fat Caesar salad dressing

2 tomatoes, cut into wedges

¼ cup chopped parsley

1. In large skillet, combine rice, chicken broth and ½ cup water. Bring to a boil. Cover; reduce heat and simmer 12 minutes.

2. Add green onions and peas to rice pilaf. Season to taste with salt and pepper. Place fish fillets on pilaf. Spoon salad dressing onto fillets. Cover and cook over low heat 8 minutes or until fish flakes when tested with a fork and rice is tender.

3. Garnish with tomatoes and parsley.   *Makes 4 servings*

Nutrition Information Per Serving: Calories: 323, Protein: 23 g, Carbohydrate: 50 g, Fat: 3 g, Cholesterol: 50 mg, Sodium: 452 mg

Variation

Orange roughy fillets or swordfish steaks can be substituted for sole fillets.

Rice and Turkey Skillet Curry

APPLE PECAN CHICKEN ROLL-UPS

½ cup apple juice

½ cup **UNCLE BEN'S®
Brand Instant Brown
Rice**

½ cup finely chopped
unpeeled apple

¼ cup chopped pecans

3 tablespoons sliced green
onions

4 boneless, skinless
chicken breasts
(about 1 pound)

1 tablespoon vegetable oil

1. Heat oven to 400°F. In small saucepan, bring apple juice to a boil. Add rice; cover, reduce heat and simmer 8 to 10 minutes or until liquid is absorbed. Stir in apple, pecans and green onions. Remove from heat.

2. Flatten each chicken breast to about ¼-inch thickness by pounding between two pieces of waxed paper. Place ¼ of rice mixture on each chicken breast. Roll up, tucking in edges. Secure with toothpicks.

3. Heat oil in medium skillet over medium-high heat. Add chicken and cook 4 to 5 minutes or until lightly browned; place in shallow baking pan. Bake 20 to 25 minutes or until chicken is no longer pink in center.   *Makes 4 servings*

Nutrition Information Per Serving: Calories: 319, Protein: 28 g, Carbohydrate: 25 g, Fat: 12 g, Cholesterol: 69 mg, Sodium: 62 mg

COOK'S TIP

For this recipe, choose an apple variety that will retain its shape when cooked, such as Granny Smith, Golden Delicious or Jonathan.

Apple Pecan Chicken Roll-Up

SHRIMP AND RICE SALAD

1 (2-cup) bag
UNCLE BEN'S® Brand
Boil-in-Bag Rice
1¼ cups snow peas
½ pound cooked peeled,
deveined shrimp
1 cup sliced celery
½ cup reduced-fat
mayonnaise
½ cup thinly sliced carrot
½ cup diced red bell pepper
1 tablespoon fresh lemon
juice

1. Cook rice according to package directions. Rinse under cold running water to cool; drain.

2. Meanwhile, slice snow peas into 1-inch lengths. In a medium bowl, combine snow peas and remaining ingredients.

3. Add cooked rice; mix well. Serve immediately or chill until ready to serve.

Makes 4 servings

Nutrition Information Per Serving: Calories: 502, Protein: 18 g, Carbohydrate: 84 g, Fat: 9 g, Cholesterol: 97 mg, Sodium: 167 mg

NEW ORLEANS GUMBO-STYLE CHICKEN

8 boneless, skinless
chicken tenderloins,
cut into 1-inch pieces
2 cans (14½ ounces) diced
tomatoes with green
pepper and onion,
undrained
2 cups water
1 box UNCLE BEN'S®
Brand Red Bean &
Rice Hearty Soup
½ teaspoon hot pepper
sauce, or to taste
1 package (10 ounces)
frozen okra

1. In large saucepan, combine chicken, tomatoes, water, soup mix, contents of seasoning packet and hot pepper sauce; mix well. Bring to a boil. Reduce heat and simmer, uncovered, 10 minutes.

2. Add okra; continue cooking 8 to 10 minutes or until chicken is no longer pink and okra is tender.   *Makes 4 servings*

Nutrition Information Per Serving: Calories: 282, Protein: 21 g, Carbohydrate: 38 g, Fat: 7 g, Cholesterol: 13 mg, Sodium: 1033 mg

Shrimp and Rice Salad

TRADITIONAL CHICKEN AND RICE

1 tablespoon olive oil
4 boneless, skinless chicken breasts (about 1 pound)
2¼ cups water
1 box COUNTRY INN® Brand Chicken Rice Dishes
½ cup chopped red bell pepper
½ cup frozen peas, thawed
¼ cup Parmesan cheese

1. Heat oil in large skillet. Add chicken; cook over medium-high heat 10 to 15 minutes or until lightly browned on both sides.

2. Add water, rice, contents of seasoning packet, bell pepper and peas; mix well. Bring to a boil. Cover; reduce heat and simmer 10 minutes or until chicken is no longer pink in center. Remove from heat. Sprinkle with cheese; let stand covered 5 minutes or until liquid is absorbed.

Makes 4 servings

Nutrition Information Per Serving: Calories: 370, Protein: 33 g, Carbohydrate: 37 g, Fat: 9 g, Cholesterol: 74 mg, Sodium: 945 mg

BEEF STROGANOFF WITH RICE

½ cup UNCLE BEN'S® CONVERTED® Brand Rice
12 ounces sirloin steak
1 teaspoon olive oil
1 small onion, sliced
2 cups sliced mushrooms
½ cup reduced-fat sour cream
¼ teaspoon dill weed
½ cup sliced green onions

1. Cook rice according to package directions.

2. Meanwhile, cut beef into thin strips. Heat oil in large skillet over medium heat. Add beef, onion and mushrooms. Cook and stir 5 minutes or until beef is cooked through. Add sour cream, dill weed and cooked rice.

3. Garnish stroganoff with green onions.

Makes 4 servings

Nutrition Information Per Serving: Calories: 252, Protein: 20 g, Carbohydrate: 25 g, Fat: 7 g, Cholesterol: 58 mg, Sodium: 59 mg

Traditional Chicken and Rice

RICE AND CHICKEN WRAPS

8 boneless, skinless
    chicken tenderloins
2 cups water
1 box UNCLE BEN'S®
    Brand Long Grain &
    Wild Rice Fast
    Cooking Recipe
½ cup reduced-fat ranch
    salad dressing
1 cup shredded lettuce
8 (10-inch) flour tortillas

1. Spray large skillet with nonstick cooking spray. Add chicken; cook over medium-high heat 10 to 12 minutes or until lightly browned on both sides. Add water, rice and contents of seasoning packet. Bring to a boil. Cover; reduce heat and simmer 5 minutes or until chicken is no longer pink in center and liquid is absorbed. Stir in salad dressing.

2. Spoon rice mixture evenly down center of each tortilla; top with lettuce. Fold in both sides of tortillas; roll up tortilla tightly from bottom, keeping filling firmly packed. Slice each wrap diagonally into 2 pieces.

Makes 4 servings

Nutrition Information Per Serving: Calories: 490, Protein: 23 g, Carbohydrate: 73 g, Fat: 12 g, Cholesterol: 31 mg, Sodium: 1368 mg

GARLIC HERB CHICKEN AND RICE SKILLET

4 boneless, skinless
    chicken breasts
    (about 1 pound)
1¾ cups water
1 box UNCLE BEN'S®
    Brand Chicken Rice
    Dishes
2 cups frozen broccoli,
    carrots and
    cauliflower medley
¼ cup garlic and herb
    flavored soft
    spreadable cheese

1. In large skillet, combine chicken, water and contents of seasoning packet, reserving rice. Bring to a boil. Reduce heat; cover and simmer 10 minutes.

2. Add rice, vegetables and cheese. Cook covered 10 to 15 minutes or until chicken is no longer pink in center. Remove from heat; let stand 5 minutes or until liquid is absorbed.

Makes 4 servings

Nutrition Information Per Serving: Calories: 331, Protein: 31 g, Carbohydrate: 39 g, Fat: 5 g, Cholesterol: 74 mg, Sodium: 955 mg

Rice and Chicken Wraps

BROCCOLI, CHICKEN AND RICE CASSEROLE

1 box UNCLE BEN'S®
    Brand Broccoli au
    Gratin Rice Dishes
2 cups boiling water
4 boneless, skinless
    chicken breasts
    (about 1 pound)
¼ teaspoon garlic powder
2 cups frozen broccoli,
    thawed
1 cup (4 ounces) reduced-
    fat shredded Cheddar
    cheese

1. Heat oven to 425°F. In 13×9-inch baking pan, combine rice and contents of seasoning packet. Add boiling water; mix well. Add chicken; sprinkle with garlic powder. Cover and bake 30 minutes.

2. Add broccoli and cheese; continue to bake, covered, 8 to 10 minutes or until chicken is no longer pink in center.

Makes 4 servings

Nutrition Information Per Serving: Calories: 383, Protein: 39 g, Carbohydrate: 38 g, Fat: 9 g, Cholesterol: 27 mg, Sodium: 1096 mg

FIESTA SOUP

6 boneless, skinless
    chicken tenderloins,
    cut into 1-inch pieces
2 cans (14½ ounces) low-
    sodium chicken broth
1 can (15 ounces) kidney
    beans, undrained
1 cup salsa
1 cup frozen corn
½ cup UNCLE BEN'S®
    Brand Instant Rice
⅓ cup shredded Monterey
    Jack cheese

1. In large saucepan, combine chicken, broth, kidney beans, salsa and corn.

2. Bring to a boil. Reduce heat and simmer uncovered 5 to 10 minutes or until chicken is no longer pink. Stir in rice. Cover; remove from heat and let stand covered 5 minutes. Top each serving with cheese.   *Makes 4 servings*

Nutrition Information Per Serving: Calories: 281, Protein: 24 g, Carbohydrate: 41 g, Fat: 5 g, Cholesterol: 31 mg, Sodium: 1349 mg

Broccoli, Chicken and Rice Casserole

Apple Pecan Chicken Roll-Ups, 82
Asian Beef Wraps, 44

BBQ Pork Stir-Fry, 14
Beef
 Asian Beef Wraps, 44
 Beef Stroganoff with Rice, 86
 Beef Tenderloins in Wild Mushroom Sauce, 40
 Burgundy Beef Stew, 12
 5-Minute Beef & Asparagus Stir-Fry, 33
 Grilled Caribbean Steak with Tropical Rice, 34
 Hearty Beef and Mushroom Soup, 16
 Stuffed Mexican Pizza Pie, 52
Broccoli, Chicken and Rice Casserole, 90

Caribbean Pork Kabobs and Rice, 78
Chicken
 Apple Pecan Chicken Roll-Ups, 82
 Broccoli, Chicken and Rice Casserole, 90
 Cajun Chicken Bayou, 10
 Cheesy Chicken Quesadillas, 57
 Chicken Casserole Olé, 54
 Chicken di Napolitano, 17
 Chicken Wellington, 13
 Classic Chicken Biscuit Pie, 22
 Drumstick & Rice Bake, 60
 Fiesta Soup, 90
 Garlic Herb Chicken and Rice Skillet, 88
 Hearty One-Pot Chicken Stew, 10
 Indian Summer Chicken and Rice Salad, 41
 Mexican Lasagna, 62
 Monterey Chicken and Rice Quiche, 38
 New Orleans Gumbo-Style Chicken, 84
 Northwoods Mushroom Swiss Melts, 23
 Pocket Meals on the Run, 63
 Rice and Chicken Wraps, 88
 Simple Stir-Fry, 58
 Southern BBQ Chicken and Rice, 63
 Sweet and Sour Rice Bowl, 51
 Traditional Chicken and Rice, 86
 Warm Spinach and Rice Chicken Salad, 37
 Zesty Island Chicken Kabobs, 47
Cool-as-a-Cucumber Salad, 76
Cornish Hens
 Cranberry-Glazed Cornish Hens with Wild Rice, 36
 Mediterranean Cornish Hens, 26
Cranberry-Glazed Cornish Hens with Wild Rice, 36

Drumstick & Rice Bake, 60

Fiesta Soup, 90
5-Minute Beef & Asparagus Stir-Fry, 33
Fried Rice Cakes, 64

Garlic Herb Chicken and Rice Skillet, 88
Grilled Caribbean Steak with Tropical Rice, 34

Grilled Fish, Vegetable & Rice Packets, 28
Grilled Swordfish Steaks, 50
Grilled Vegetables & Brown Rice, 74

Ham: Ham & Asparagus Brunch Bake, 48
Hearty Beef and Mushroom Soup, 16
Hearty One-Pot Chicken Stew, 10

Indian Summer Chicken and Rice Salad, 41
Italian Sausage and Rice Frittata, 20

Mediterranean Cornish Hens, 26
Mexican Lasagna, 62
Monterey Chicken and Rice Quiche, 38

New Orleans Gumbo-Style Chicken, 84
Northwoods Mushroom Swiss Melts, 23

Pocket Meals on the Run, 63
Pork (see also **Ham, Sausage)**
 BBQ Pork Stir-Fry, 14
 Caribbean Pork Kabobs and Rice, 78
 Southwest Pork & Rice, 32

Quick Fried Rice, 73
Quick Skillet Quiche, 72

Rice & Artichoke Phyllo Triangles, 30
Rice and Chicken Wraps, 88
Rice and Chick-Pea Chili, 66
Rice and Turkey Skillet Curry, 80
Rice & Vegetable Salad, 68
Rice and Veggie Cheese Medley, 56
Rice, Cheese & Bean Enchiladas, 70
Rice Pilaf with Fish Fillets, 80
Roasted Turkey Breast with Cherry & Apple Rice Stuffing, 46

Sausage: Italian Sausage and Rice Frittata, 20
Seafood
 Grilled Fish, Vegetables & Rice Packets, 28
 Grilled Swordfish Steaks, 50
 Rice Pilaf with Fish Fillets, 80
 Shrimp and Rice Salad, 84
 Thai Seafood Kabobs with Spicy Rice, 42
 Warm Mediterranean Rice Salad, 24
 Wild Rice Shrimp Paella, 18
Simple Stir-Fry, 58
Southern BBQ Chicken and Rice, 63
Southwest Pork & Rice, 32
Stuffed Mexican Pizza Pie, 52
Sweet and Sour Rice Bowl, 51

Tex-Mex Rice Salad, 73
Thai Seafood Kabobs with Spicy Rice, 42
Traditional Chicken and Rice, 86
Turkey
 Rice and Turkey Skillet Curry, 80
 Roasted Turkey Breast with Cherry & Apple Rice Stuffing, 46
 Wild Rice Meatball Primavera, 8

UNCLE BEN'S® Brand Black Beans & Rice
Vegetarian Rice & Black Bean Chili, 68
UNCLE BEN'S® Brand Boil-in-Bag Rice
BBQ Pork Stir-Fry, 14
Rice, Cheese & Bean Enchiladas, 70
Shrimp and Rice Salad, 84
Simple Stir-Fry, 58
Sweet and Sour Rice Bowl, 51
Zesty Island Chicken Kabobs, 47
**UNCLE BEN'S® Brand Broccoli au Gratin Rice
Dishes:** Broccoli, Chicken and Rice
Casserole, 90
**UNCLE BEN'S® Brand Brown & Wild Rice
Mushroom Recipe**
5-Minute Beef & Asparagus Stir-Fry, 33
Hearty Beef and Mushroom Soup, 16
Wild Rice Pesto Timbales, 29
UNCLE BEN'S® Brand Brown Rice: Grilled
Vegetables & Brown Rice, 74
UNCLE BEN'S® Brand Cheese Rice Dishes:
Rice and Veggie Cheese Medley, 56
**UNCLE BEN'S® Brand Chicken & Broccoli Rice
Dishes:** Monterey Chicken and Rice
Quiche, 38
UNCLE BEN'S® Brand Chicken Rice Dishes
Cheesy Chicken Quesadillas, 57
Classic Chicken Biscuit Pie, 22
Garlic Herb Chicken and Rice Skillet, 88
Traditional Chicken and Rice, 86
Warm Spinach and Rice Chicken Salad,
37
**UNCLE BEN'S® Brand Homestyle Chicken &
Vegetables Rice Dishes**
Drumstick & Rice Bake, 60
Fried Rice Cakes, 64
UNCLE BEN'S® Brand Instant Brown Rice
Apple Pecan Chicken Roll-Ups, 82
Italian Sausage and Rice Frittata, 20
Quick Fried Rice, 73
UNCLE BEN'S® Brand Instant Rice
Asian Beef Wraps, 44
Chicken Casserole Olé, 54
Chicken Wellington, 13
Fiesta Soup, 90
Indian Summer Chicken and Rice Salad, 41
Mediterranean Cornish Hens, 26
Pocket Meals on the Run, 63
Quick Skillet Quiche, 72
Stuffed Mexican Pizza Pie, 52
Tex-Mex Rice Salad, 73
**UNCLE BEN'S® Brand Long Grain & Wild
Butter & Herb Rice**
Beef Tenderloins in Wild Mushroom Sauce, 40
Rice & Artichoke Phyllo Triangles, 30
Wild Rice Shrimp Paella, 18
**UNCLE BEN'S® Brand Long Grain & Wild
Rice Fast Cooking Recipe**
Cranberry-Glazed Cornish Hens with Wild
Rice, 36
Rice and Chicken Wraps, 88
Wild Rice Meatball Primavera, 8

**UNCLE BEN'S® Brand Long Grain & Wild
Rice Original Recipe**
Grilled Fish, Vegetables & Rice Packets, 28
Ham & Asparagus Brunch Bake, 48
Northwoods Mushroom Swiss Melts, 23
**UNCLE BEN'S® Brand Long Grain & Wild
Vegetable & Herb Rice:** Roasted Turkey
Breast with Cherry & Apple Rice Stuffing,
46
**UNCLE BEN'S® Brand Pinto Beans &
Rice:** Mexican Lasagna, 62
UNCLE BEN'S® Brand Red Beans & Rice
Cajun Chicken Bayou, 10
Hearty One-Pot Chicken Stew, 10
**UNCLE BEN'S® Brand Red Bean & Rice
Hearty Soup:** New Orleans Gumbo-Style
Chicken, 84
UNCLE BEN'S® Brand Rice Pilaf Dishes
Burgundy Beef Stew, 12
Chicken di Napolitano, 17
UNCLE BEN'S® CONVERTED® Brand Rice
Beef Stroganoff with Rice, 86
Caribbean Pork Kabobs and Rice, 78
Cool-as-a-Cucumber Salad, 76
Grilled Caribbean Steak with Tropical Rice, 34
Grilled Swordfish Steaks, 50
Rice and Chick-Pea Chili, 66
Rice and Turkey Skillet Curry, 80
Rice & Vegetable Salad, 68
Rice Pilaf with Fish Fillets, 80
Southern BBQ Chicken and Rice, 63
Southwest Pork & Rice, 32
Thai Seafood Kabobs with Spicy Rice, 42
Warm Mediterranean Rice Salad, 24

Vegetarian Rice & Black Bean Chili, 68

Warm Mediterranean Rice Salad, 24
Warm Spinach and Rice Chicken Salad, 37
Wild Rice Meatball Primavera, 8
Wild Rice Pesto Timbales, 29
Wild Rice Shrimp Paella, 18

Zesty Island Chicken Kabobs, 47

METRIC CONVERSION CHART

VOLUME MEASUREMENTS (dry)

⅛ teaspoon = 0.5 mL

¼ teaspoon = 1 mL

½ teaspoon = 2 mL

¾ teaspoon = 4 mL

1 teaspoon = 5 mL

1 tablespoon = 15 mL

2 tablespoons = 30 mL

¼ cup = 60 mL

⅓ cup = 75 mL

½ cup = 125 mL

⅔ cup = 150 mL

¾ cup = 175 mL

1 cup = 250 mL

2 cups = 1 pint = 500 mL

3 cups = 750 mL

4 cups = 1 quart = 1 L

VOLUME MEASUREMENTS (fluid)

1 fluid ounce (2 tablespoons) = 30 mL

4 fluid ounces (½ cup) = 125 mL

8 fluid ounces (1 cup) = 250 mL

12 fluid ounces (1½ cups) = 375 mL

16 fluid ounces (2 cups) = 500 mL

WEIGHTS (mass)

½ ounce = 15 g

1 ounce = 30 g

3 ounces = 90 g

4 ounces = 120 g

8 ounces = 225 g

10 ounces = 285 g

12 ounces = 360 g

16 ounces = 1 pound = 450 g

DIMENSIONS

1/16 inch = 2 mm

⅛ inch = 3 mm

¼ inch = 6 mm

½ inch = 1.5 cm

¾ inch = 2 cm

1 inch = 2.5 cm

OVEN TEMPERATURES

250°F = 120°C

275°F = 140°C

300°F = 150°C

325°F = 160°C

350°F = 180°C

375°F = 190°C

400°F = 200°C

425°F = 220°C

450°F = 230°C

BAKING PAN SIZES

Utensil	Size in Inches/ Quarts	Metric Volume	Size in Centimeters
Baking or Cake Pan (square or rectangular)	8×8×2	2 L	20×20×5
	9×9×2	2.5 L	23×23×5
	12×8×2	3 L	30×20×5
	13×9×2	3.5 L	33×23×5
Loaf Pan	8×4×3	1.5 L	20×10×7
	9×5×3	2 L	23×13×7
Round Layer Cake Pan	8×1½	1.2 L	20×4
	9×1½	1.5 L	23×4
Pie Plate	8×1¼	750 mL	20×3
	9×1¼	1 L	23×3
Baking Dish or Casserole	1 quart	1 L	—
	1½ quart	1.5 L	—
	2 quart	2 L	—